BREADFRUIT RECIPES

Breadfruit Recipes

ISBN 978-1-257-44654-4

Contents:

Foreword. .... 1.

Bacon Twists .... 4.

Balls and Sticks .... 7.

Bread de B'fruit. (Loaf) .... 10.

Cake .... 12.

Chicken Swiss Roll .... 14.

Chips (Zesty) .... 18.

Cottage Breadfruit .... 20.

Delight .... 23.

Duchess .... 25.

Hash .... 27.

Lasagna .... 29.

National Dish .... 32.

Pie .... 37.

Pizza Avec B'fruit .... 39.

Pudding .... 41.

Salad .... 43.

Salt Fish, Pig Tail & Rice .... 45.

Stew .... 49.
Sweet & Sour Glazed B'fruit .... 53.
Zesty Cheese Casserole .... 55.
Summary ....57.

Foreword

The idea of this book 'Breadfruit Recipes 'is to encourage more appreciation of the fruit from the plant that Captain Bligh of 'Mutiny on the Bounty' fame, struggled to transport form the 'South Pacific, to the Caribbean, way back around 1787.

Today the breadfruit grows widely across the Caribbean region but not utilized as much as it can be, due to forms of eating stigma. However, the breadfruit has high nutritional value and potential to be: cooked, fried or baked into cost effective meals and during a period when the price of eating perpetually moves upward.

Where the word; 'Breadfruit' or some derivation of it does not appear in the title of any recipe; it should be assumed as the first word of that heading and is intended to precede that stated heading. For example the title: "Cake" means: 'Breadfruit Cake'.

The developer and author rotate cooking duties weekly. My cooking strategy is to prepare meals that are twice the quantity of what we consume at the first sitting. Half is used on the day of preparation; the other half is transferred into an oven dish and stored in a refrigerator for two or three days as the case maybe. Days when it is planned to use the second portion; the dish containing the saved food is removed from the refrigerator about four hours prior to heating in an oven set to about 300 degrees for thirty minutes.

It has been our experience that the taste and quality of the second serving is usually much improved compared to the first. (Somewhat like, a good wine that ages with time.)

Some of the included recipes, were developed by the author, however, the majority of dishes were thought of, designed and perfected by my wife. In those instances, my role was the number one taster and quality advisor. A task where the only danger was occasionally overeating, especially when self-control got to be overtaken by the excitement of drooling taste-buds.

Our thanks to Delores Audain who willingly acted as my assistant taster and gave valuable service in that department.

The author and also the developer of dishes contained in this book, sincerely hope that attempts at creating the various suggestions will prove exciting, delicious and enjoyable combinations as we have found the to be.

Happy cooking to all and better still, enjoy eating your results.

Bon Appetite!!

Avis Nathan

Researcher and developer.

Samuel Nathan,

Author and zealously enthusiastic guinea pig.

<u>Bacon Twists.</u>

Ingredients:

1 lb. of full Breadfruit.

1 Tablespoon of Vinegar.

1 Tablespoon of Vegetable Oil.

2 Tablespoons of La-Choy sauce.

1 Teaspoon of prepared Mustard.

1 Tablespoon of Brown Sugar or Honey.

2 Grated Garlic Cloves.

1 Tablespoons of Mixed Seasoning (From the Kitchen of Avis Nathan).

2 Teaspoons of Hot Pepper Sauce (From the Kitchen of Avis Nathan).

1 Teaspoon of salt.

6 Slices of Bacon.

¼ Cup of Ketchup.

Method:

Wash the breadfruit in its skin, place it in a pot, cover the contents with tap water, add the salt, vinegar and vegetable oil then cook until tender, taking care not to over-cook the breadfruit.

Once cooked, throw off the liquid and cool the breadfruit using tap water.

Create 6 boat-shapes from the breadfruit (each of 2 inch base width).

Then cut each boat in two diagonal parts.

Divide each slice of bacon into two halves lengthwise, then allow them to thaw until they become manageable.

Combine the other ingredients into a medium sized bowl, whisk them together then set aside for basting later.

Take each diagonal slice of breadfruit, using a ½ slice of bacon, begin one inch from the top of the breadfruit and finish one inch from the bottom. Wrap the bacon around the breadfruit, top to bottom, stretching slightly while in the process of wrapping. Also, ensure that at the end of each bacon wrap, the lose end lies under the breadfruit slice to prevent it tilting.

Place the bacon-twists on top of an un-greased baking sheet and place in a hot oven, set to 300 degrees for ten minutes.

Remove the twists from the oven and using the Ketchup mixture, brush the twists all over then return to the oven.

After ten minutes, remove the twists and turn them, taking care not to loosen the bacon ends.

Brush the twists with the mixture once more before returning them to the oven for another 10 to 15 minutes or until they attain the golden colour of choice.

Serve at any temperature.

These are delicious as a side dish or 'finger goodies'. They are also very nice with a chilled glass of your favourite wine, port, sherry. Especially so with a glass of iced Juke (From the Kitchen of Avis Nathan).

Balls and Sticks.

Ingredients:

1 Cup of grated breadfruit.

3 Teaspoons of baking powder.

½ Teaspoon of baking soda.

1 Tablespoon of grated onions.

1 Tablespoon of Margarine.

1½ Cups of flour.

1 Teaspoon of salt.

¾ cup of water.

Method:

Sift into a large bowl: flour, baking powder, baking soda and salt. Add the grated breadfruit and onions.

Mix the contents well until the mixture becomes crumbly.

Gradually add small amounts of water, ensuring that the 'dough' does not over-wet.

Knead the contents well to achieve good elasticity.

Allow the mixture to stand between 10 to 15 minutes.

Push the risen dough down to its original level and leave a further 10 minutes.

Separate the dough into balls and stick portions.

Balls:

Cut into required sizes then roll to shape in the style of dumplings or 'Johnny Cakes'.

Fry in hot oil (recycled perhaps) until the balls are golden.

These are delicious when used as a breakfast aide.

Sticks:

Place the mixture on a slightly floured surface and roll out to a consistency of around ½ -inch thickness.

Place the sheet of dough on a flat baking surface then into the oven set to 250 degrees.

Allow to bake for around 15 minutes.

Remove the baked slab from the oven, butter the top and sprinkle with Parmesan Cheese.

Bake for another 10 – 15 minutes or until the top is nicely golden.

Whilst the slab is hot, cut into 1-inch thick strips then cut those strips into lengths of your choice.

These sticks are very enjoyable when

accompanied

with a chilled glass of **'JUKE'** (From the Kitchen of Avis Nathan).

Bread de B'fruit. (Loaf)

Ingredients:

3 Cups of sifted flour. 2 Teaspoons of yeast.

1½ Cups of ripe mashed breadfruit. 2 Teaspoons of salt

4 Ozs. of margarine/shortening. 1 Teaspoon of (brown

¾ Cup of warm water. Sugar).

Greased baking bread pan.

Method:

In a '¼ cup' of warm water, add sugar, yeast and stir until both are dissolved.

Leave for about ten minutes until it begins to rise.

Combine the flour, salt, margarine and mashed breadfruit in a large mixing bowl. Stir the combination gently at first, then with clean fingers.

Add the yeast mixture, ½ cup of water and salt.

Mix the contents together then knead with your fingers until the dough gets to be elastic and firm.

Cover the dough for one hour then re-knead it for about five to ten minutes.

Cover and leave to stand for another ½ hour.

Spread a thin cover of flour on a clean surface and place the dough on it.

Turn the dough over the floured-surface until completely covered with the new flour.

Fit it into a properly sized baking bread pan.

Place the tin and contents in an oven set to 300 degrees and bake for 30 to 40 minutes or until the finished bread is golden.

Cake

Ingredients:

1½ Cups of ripe breadfruit mashed.
4 Oz's. of butter or margarine.
1 Cup of flour heaped.
2 Teaspoons of baking powder.
½ Teaspoon baking soda.
½ Cup condensed milk.
4 Eggs.
½ Cup vegetable oil.
¼ Cup of white sugar
¼ Teaspoon of salt.
2 Teaspoons of (vanilla Essence).

Method:

Using a suitably sized mixing bowl combine: butter/margarine, sugar, condensed milk, eggs, oil and vanilla essence.

Sift: flour, baking powder, baking soda and salt together. Carefully spoon into the mixing bowl and mix until the mixture is smooth.

Grease then thinly flour a cake tin before pouring the contents of the mixing bowl into it.

Bake in an oven set to 350 degrees for 30 to 35 minutes or

a toothpick is clean when removed from the cake after testing.

Chicken Swiss Roll.

Ingredients:

2 lbs. Breadfruit (very full) 2 Eggs, beaten.

2 Ozs. Butter/margarine. + 2 tablespoons extra.

2 Medium sized onions. 3 Garlic cloves.

1 Teaspoon of thyme. 1 – 2 Sprig of herbs.

1 lb. of minced chicken (beef, pork or mutton).

½ Cup of toasted bread crumbs.

1 Tablespoon & 1 teaspoon of salt.

3 Tablespoons of evaporated milk.

1 Tablespoon of dry mustard.

2 Ozs. & 2 Tablespoons of flour.

2 @ 18" lengths of wax paper.

2 Tablespoons of vegetable oil.

1 each of red, green & yellow sweet peppers.

1 Tablespoon of Hot Pepper Sauce (From the Kitchen of Avis Nathan)

Method:

Wash, peel and separate the edible portion of the breadfruit.

Cut it into manageable chunks and place in a suitable sized

pot.

Cover the contents with tap water and cook for 15 – 20 minutes.

Meanwhile, chop: peppers, onions, garlic, herbs and mix together.

Place a heavy doving dish with oil onto a high flame/heat.

Scrape the mixture into the 'doving' dish when it is very hot and stir continuously.

Add the chicken and blend together with the Hot Sauce.

Once the mixture blends to satisfaction, remove form the heat and set aside.

By which time, the breadfruit should have cooked to the required consistency.

Strain off the boiling water.

Add to the boiled breadfruit: 2 Oz's. of butter/margarine, milk, mustard and the teaspoon of salt.

Mash the items together well until there are no lumps in

the mixture.

Add the 2 Oz's. of flour and mix vigorously for 3 – 4 minutes.

Set the mixture in a refrigerator for at least 20 minutes.

Arrange the two lengths of wax paper beside each other with a '4 inch' overlap.

Sprinkle one tablespoon of flour over the wax paper, place breadfruit dough onto the paper, spread with fingers, lengthways and across leaving: four inch border on the short edge furthest away; no border at the closest short edge; the two long edges should have borders of 2 ½ inches each.

Flatten the dough with a rolling pin to ½-inch thickness.

Drain excess juices from the relish mixture into a vessel for later use and spread the mixture along the dough evenly; leaving 1 inch edge between the dough and relish at the two long side edges; four inch space of the relish on the dough at the far short edge and no space at the close short edge.

Lift the paper with the closest short edge and roll it towards the far edge, for about three inches.

Peel the paper backwards and continue to roll – peel paper back after each roll cycle, to the end of the dough. Using a fork, mix the breadcrumbs in a bowl with 2 tablespoons of margarine until it is crumbly, sprinkle it onto the roll and bake in a moderate oven (250 degrees) for twenty five to thirty minutes.

Continuously applied, the creative process should take about one hour.

Chips

(Zesty).

Ingredients:

1/3 of a very full breadfruit.

1 Tablespoon of salt.

1 Tablespoon of vegetable oil.

1 Tablespoon of vinegar.

1 Egg beaten.

¼ Cup of milk.

½ Cup of water.

½ Cup of flour.

1 Crushed garlic clove.

4 Cups of Chip frying oil.

2 Tablespoons of 'Zesty Italian Dressing'.

1 Teaspoon of prepared mustard.

2 Teaspoons of Hot Pepper Sauce. (From the Kitchen of Avis Nathan).

Method:

Cover the breadfruit with water, in its skin, add ½ tablespoon of vegetable oil and ½ tablespoon of salt then boil until the breadfruit can be pierced with a toothpick. Take care not to overcook the breadfruit. After cooking, reduce the temperature of the breadfruit under a running water tap. Peel off the skin and cut out the guts. Slice the edible portion into wedge-like -chip shapes. Cover a breadboard with a thin layer of flour. Place the breadfruit chips on the floured board and roll with a rolling pin or clean empty bottle then set aside.

Except for the 'Chip Frying Oil', Combine, the remaining ingredients into a large, shallow bowl.

Blend the mixture together.

Heat the Chip Frying Oil to about 300 degrees.

Dip each stick of chip in the batter before placing it into the hot oil.

Fry until golden brown then remove each chip and place onto a platter covered with two layers of paper towels.

For more delicious results, drizzle a little Italian dressing of your choice over the finished chips.

Cottage Breadfruit

Ingredients:

1 Young-full breadfruit. 1 Pack of bacon strips.

10.5 oz. tin of baked beans. 2 oz. Margarine.

½ Teaspoon of salt.

1 lb. Minced meat, (beef, pork, chicken or mutton).

2 Tablespoons of 'Mixed Seasoning' (From the Kitchen of Avis Nathan).

1 Teaspoon of 'Hot Pepper Sauce' (From the Kitchen of Avis Nathan).

Method

Cut the breadfruit in two halves, place both in a suitable sized pot and cover with water.

Boil the breadfruit until it feels tender to the prod of a kitchen or dining fork.

Cut the entire breadfruit into boats, peel the boats and remove the un-edible internal parts.

Shave the useful boats into slices, each slice of about 5 – 7 millimeters thick.

Use the margarine to

grease the inside of a medium sized baking dish.

Cover the greased dish base with the first layer of sliced breadfruit, placing the slices close to each other.

Spread the minced meat evenly over the first layer of breadfruit, ensuring that it is completely covered.

Place the next layer of breadfruit over the minced meat.

The fourth layer will be the baked beans, also spread evenly.

The fifth layer is another breadfruit one.

For the sixth layer, place slices of bacon strips, lengthwise around the dish, shortening the lengths to fit into the smaller spaces as the bacon reaches the center.

Mix the hot-sauce, seasoning and salt together. Then spread it over the bacon layer.

Place the remaining breadfruit slices at even intervals on the seasoned spread.

Place the dish of contents in an oven set at 250 degrees for thirty minutes, then reduce the oven heat to 150 degrees for a further ten minutes.

Serve the Cottage Pie hot, with chilled Chablis or low alcohol 'Arbor Mist' for premium enjoyment.

Delight

Ingredients:

1 Ripe Breadfruit.	8 Oz's of Bacon.
1 cup of milk.	1 Chopped onion.
1 Finely chopped tomato.	2 Oz's of cheese.
Available Sweet peppers.	2 Sprigs of parsley.

Salt and pepper to taste.

2 Tablespoons of butter or margarine.

Method:

Fry the bacon in a pan until crisply done.

Remove the bacon from the pan, sauté the onions and tomatoes then set them aside.

Peal, cut the edible part of the breadfruit into small pieces, wash and then cook them until they are tender.

Drain the liquid from the cooked breadfruit.

Mash the breadfruit, add butter/margarine, milk and bacon, then stir thoroughly.

Add eggs, sautéed onions, tomatoes and mix well.

Sprinkle in the salt and pepper.

Transfer the mixture into a greased dish and bake for 45 minutes.

Tuck the parsley into the most convenient corner between the dish and Breadfruit Delight.

Duchess

Ingredients:

1 Full breadfruit.

½ Teaspoon of salt.

½ Cup of Evaporated Milk.

1 Tablespoon of Vegetable Oil.

3 Medium sized carrots, sliced and washed.

6 Oz's of butter or margarine(melted).

½ Teaspoon of Hot Pepper Sauce (From the Kitchen of Avis Nathan).

3 Eggs' yolks.

12 Oz's of peas.

Method:

Peel, wash, cut to size and boil the breadfruit until it is tender and ready to mash. Take about 2 pounds or 6 cups of mashed breadfruit for the dish. Beat the egg yolks together with ½ cup of butter or margarine, salt and milk. Thoroughly stir it into the mashed breadfruit. Use a baking dish of at least, size 13 inches by 9 inches and 3 inches deep. Butter inside the dish, spread ½ of the breadfruit mixture evenly around the dish.

Pipe the remaining breadfruit mixture, through a piping

bag, into a lattice pattern over the top of the first breadfruit base in the baking dish. Drizzle, the remaining butter or margarine over the breadfruit.

Set the oven temperature to 400 – 450 degrees and bake the breadfruit for about 6 – 8 minutes or until the top is golden brown. Cook and drain the peas. Then spoon them into each lattice space.

Cook and drain the carrots, drizzle the vegetable oil over them and place around the inside perimeter of the dish.

Hash.

Ingredients:

1 Medium ripe breadfruit. 1 Large tin of corned beef.

12 Oz's. tin of baked beans. 2 Eggs.

2 Oz's. Butter or margarine.

4 Tablespoons of Mixed Seasoning (From the Kitchen of Avis Nathan).

Method:

Boil the breadfruit in the skin until it is soft enough to be mashed.

Peel off a thin layer of the outer skin, remove the inner, inedible part of the breadfruit and mash while it is still hot or warm.

Separate into two half portions: the mashed breadfruit; corned beef; baked beans. (This helps to manage the material handling).

Mix both half sets individually: breadfruit, corned beef and baked beans.

Use the butter or margarine to grease inside the baking dish.

Combine both halves of breadfruit mixtures into the

baking dish, mixing them together.

Level off the top of the mixture and create a design of your choice, using a dinner fork.

Beat the eggs together and pour over the breadfruit mixture, taking care that the eggs cover the Hash.

Bake in an oven set to 250 degrees for thirty-five minutes.

Lasagna`.

Ingredients:

1 Full breadfruit. 1 lb. Ground beef.

1 Large onion (chopped). 8 Oz's Ricotta cheese.

1 Teaspoon of crushed Oregano. 2 Eggs.

¼ Cup of Parmesan cheese. 2 Sprigs of parsley.

1 Large tin of Spaghetti sauce.

1 Pack of thinly sliced Mozzarella cheese.

Method:

Cook the breadfruit complete with skin until it can be pierced with a tooth-pick.

Cool, by running tap water over the breadfruit.

In a large enough dish, cook the ground beef, separating in the process.

Add Onions, Oregano and continue to cook for about ten minutes.

Cover the meaty substance with the spaghetti sauce, stir, then cook for another 15 minutes.

Spoon ¼ of the sauce mixture along the bottom of a baking dish (13" x 9" and 2" deep).

Peel the breadfruit and slice it into 28 parts.

Arrange '7' breadfruit slices over the sauce, flat side down.

Combine the Ricotta Cheese with the eggs, mixing them well.

Spoon on, ¼ of the 'Ricotta Cheese – eggs' mixture and another ¼ of the remaining sauce.

Arrange another '7' breadfruit slices' layer; cover that layer with another ¼ of 'Ricotta Cheese – eggs' mixture and portion of sauce.

Continue for another two layers until all the breadfruit slices, Ricotta mixture and sauce are used.

Crumble the Mozzarella Cheese over the top of the uncooked Lasagna.

Sprinkle the Parmesan Cheese over the Mozzarella topping.

Bake in a moderate oven for between 45 and 50 minutes or until the contents get bubbly hot.

Garnish with the parsley.

Allow to cool for about 20 minutes before serving.

Lasagna standing by a cold glass of Juke!

(From the Kitchen of Avis Nathan)

National Dish

Stewed Salt-fish

Ingredients

1 Medium sized onion. ½ lb of Tomatoes.

3Tablespoons of Cooking oil. ½ Stock Cube.

1½ Green Peppers (chopped). 2 lbs of Salt-fish.

4 Tablespoons Mixed Seasoning. (From Kitchen of Avis Nathan1Tablespoon Hot pepper sauce.(From the Kitchen of Avis Nathan).

Method:

Boil salt-fish for five minutes; throw off water and remove scales and skin according to choice. Renew water and boil until tender, remove bones according to taste. Place all items except the salt-fish into a saucepan, heat to simmering temperature with the Stock Cube crushed in the mixture. Add the stripped salt-fish into the mixture. Stir gently for one minute; then add one cup of water. Bring to the boil and allow to simmer for seven minutes. Turn off heat; cover the pan and wait to serve with other parts of the dish.

Seasoned Breadfruit.

Ingredients:

1 Tablespoon of margarine. 1 Medium sized onion.

1 Red sweet pepper diced. ½ Stock cube.

2 Tablespoons of cooking oil.

3 Breadfruit boats, diced into 1 inch cubes.

3 Tablespoon Mixed Seasoning (From the Kitchen of Avis Nathan).

1 Tablespoon of Hot Pepper Sauce (From the Kitchen of Avis Nathan).

Method:

Dissolve stock in boiled water.

Melt margarine in a saucepan over adequate heat then add cooking oil and onions. Stir frequently until onions are golden brown. Add items 4 through 7, stirring them into the mixture for ½ minute. Add the breadfruit to stock mixture and pour into cooking saucepan, gently stirring. Cook until breadfruit is tender then remove from heat. Cover the contents until ready to serve.

Corn Dumplings:

Ingredients:

The ingredients are making one dumpling. Multiply them by the number of dumplings required.

1 Tablespoon of flour. ½ Tablespoon of cornmeal.

¼ inch square of bacon rind. 1 Teaspoon oil.

1/8 Teaspoon of baking powder.

Method:

Place ingredients, except the bacon rind into a mixing bowl add small amounts of water, kneading consistently, until the consistency is firm. Create into desired shapes and push the bacon rind to its middle. Cook until they offer resistance to a fork when prodded.

Spicy Plantains:

Ingredients:

2 Oz's of Ginger.

1 Oz of Salt.

2 Tablespoons of cooking oil.

2 Plantains shaped.

1 Small grated Onion.

½ Teaspoon of Hot-sauce (From the Kitchen of Avis Nathan).

Method:

Combine the ingredients in a bowl and toss until mixed. Fry in batches until golden brown and cooked. Remove and drain on a paper towel.

Share Portions:

Place combinations according to appetite of quantities from each dish on suitable sized plates and serve, applying 'fine tuning' by adding salt and 'Hot Pepper Sauce' (From the Kitchen of Avis Nathan') to satisfy tastes.

Pie.

Ingredients:

1 lb. of ripe breadfruit. 8 Oz. tin of table cream.

1 Teaspoon of mustard. 6 Oz's of grated cheese.

1 medium onion minced. 1 Tablespoon of flour.

Sweet peppers, minced (red, green & yellow).

2 Teaspoons of Hot Pepper Sauce (From the Kitchen of Avis Nathan).

Salt to taste

Method.

Peel, wash and cook the breadfruit.

Mash the breadfruit to a fine consistency.

Add 4 ounces of grated cheese and the other items except the two ounces of grated cheese.

Mix thoroughly, pour into a greased dish then use a fork to make patterns across the top of the mixture.

Sprinkle the remaining two ounces of cheese over the top.

Bake at 250 degrees for about twenty minutes or until the pie's top is golden brown.

Pizza avec B'fruit

Ingredients:

1 Medium sized pizza (best with Pepperoni topping).

1 Young Breadfruit.

¼ lb of Butter

½ Cup of vinegar.

1 Tablespoon of salt.

¼lb of Olives.

½ large onion.

¼ Cup of vegetable oil.

Method:

Wash and boil the in-skin breadfruit with vinegar, oil and salt added to the water, just covering the breadfruit with the liquid.

When the breadfruit is pierce-able with a toothpick, remove the pot from the heat. Cool the breadfruit with ordinary tap water. Peel the breadfruit, remove the centre and cut into boats, (2 per portion).

Butter a cake pan or other baking utensil, place the 'breadfruit boats' in the baking vessel and butter the 'up – sides'.

Place the vessel in an oven at moderate temperature for 15 minutes.

Turn over the boats, return to the oven along with the pizza for a further 20 minutes.

Serve portions of pizza, 2 boats of breadfruit, olives and sliced onion rings.

To enhance the palate serve with either of the following white wines chilled (the fruitier; the better): Chablis, Lieber Frau Milch, Sancerre, Chardonnay or Prince Blanc Sauvignon.

Pudding

Ingredients:

2 Sticks of margarine (½ lb).

¼ lb. of mixed fruit.

3 Teaspoons of baking powder.

1 Teaspoon of baking soda.

2 Cups of ripe breadfruit (mashed).

2 Teaspoons of Vanilla Essence.

1 Cup of flour.

½ Cup of milk.

½ Cup of sugar.

1 Teaspoon of salt.

4 Eggs.

Method:

Mix the sugar with margarine then add: milk, breadfruit, essence and continue to mix.

Sift: flour, baking powder, baking soda and salt together; then combine with the fruits to the breadfruit mixture.

Continue to mix thoroughly, before pouring the contents into a greased 'loaf-pan'.

Bake in an oven set to 350 degrees for 35 – 40 minutes.

After baking, cool on a rack.

Tastes best when eaten warm.

Left over life can be lengthened if stored in a refrigerator.

SALAD.

Recipe`

2 Hardboiled eggs chopped. ½ Teaspoon of salt.
1 sprig of herbs, chopped. 2 Tablespoons salad oil.
1 Tablespoon of white vinegar. 1 Teaspoon dry mustard.
1 Tablespoon lemon or lime juice.
2 Cloves of garlic, crushed & chopped.
1 Medium sized onion coarsely chopped.

1 Stork of celery, chopped in ½ inch chunks.
1 Oz. green and yellow sweet peppers mixed.

¾ lb or two (2) cups of cooked – cubed (¼ inch) breadfruit (between young & full).
1 Tablespoon Hot Pepper Sauce (From the Kitchen of Avis Nathan).

Method.

Combine all ingredients in a large bowl and toss them, using two salad forks; turn salad on a well washed and dried breadfruit leaf or onto a clean plate; serve at room temperature.

Salt Fish, Pig Tail & Rice.

Ingredients:

¾ lb. of Salt Fish. ¾ lb. of Pig Tail.

1 lb. of Rice. 1 Medium Onion.

2 Pegs of Garlic. 4 Oz's of Cooking oil.

2 Tablespoons of vinegar. 4 Boats of breadfruit.

1 Tablespoon of tomato paste.

1 Tablespoon of curry powder.

4 Tablespoons of Mixed Seasoning. (From the Kitchen of Avis Nathan).

2 Teaspoons of Hot Pepper Sauce. (From the Kitchen of Avis Nathan).

Method:

Shred the salt fish and cut the pigtails into chunks. Clean then boil the 'pigtails and salt fish' in water, vinegar and ½ teaspoon of cooking oil, until the desired amount of salt is removed in the process. Note that it would be wasteful to boil out all the salt.

Chop the onions and garlic then mix with the tomato paste, curry powder, Hot

Pepper Sauce and Mixed Seasoning.

Pour the remaining oil into a 'doving dish' and add the mixture to it. Place the dish on a hot heat source and stir continuously until the onions are slightly brown. Add the pig tails and continue stirring until the pig tail begins to turn golden. Pour a ½ cup of water into the dish and allow to simmer until the pig tails can be pierced with a dinner fork, add salt fish, cook for five minutes, ensuring that the sauce does not evaporate completely. If that appears to be likely, add small amounts of water to maintain a suitable sauce level.

Wash the rice and pour in a suitable sized cooking pot, add water and bring to the boil. With the breadfruit diced, add to the boiling rice, turn the heat down to permit a slow boil, stir occasionally until the rice and breadfruit compound are of a soft yield.

Serve the rice in a plate first, place suitable portions of the salt fish and pig tail on top, then sprinkle sauce over the plate to taste.

Salt Fish, Pig Tail & Rice.

Turned into 'Bake-Up'

My meal creation policy is to prepare twice the amount needed for immediate use. That portion for later consumption is stored in an oven dish: Rice and breadfruit combination first, then the salt fish, pigtail, pouring the gravy over the contents last. The dish then goes into the refrigerator for two or three days.

When the saved meal is required, remove the dish from the

fridge about three hours before preparation. Heat at temperatures around 300 degrees, for thirty minutes and serve hot.

My experience is that, the second serving of any dish is tastier than the first.

I call the strategy: ‘Preparing two meals with one effort’ because it saves time and energy.

This is how the ‘Bake-up’ looks and it is delicious!

STEW.

In the pot.

Ingredients: (For a serving of four)

½ Teacup of butter beans. 4 Tablespoons of fine flour.

6 Oz's of Irish potatoes. ½ Teaspoon of salt.

1 Medium onion, diced. 2 Garlic cloves.

2 Tablespoons of cornmeal. 6 Ounces Sweet potatoes.

¼ Breadfruit (medium). 2 inches bacon rind (fat

part).

1 Tablespoons vegetable oil.

1 Teaspoon of Baking Powder

1lb. Stewing mutton or goat meat.

6 Ounces yam, Dasheen or Tania.

1 Tomato chopped or 2 Tablespoons of chunks.

1Tablespoon Mixed Seasoning (From the Kitchen of Avis Nathan').

2 Teaspoons Hot Pepper Sauce (From the 'Kitchen of Avis Nathan').

Method:

In a suitable boiling pot, begin with 1½ pints of water. Boil the butter beans and meat for fifteen minutes. Add 1 teaspoon of vegetable oil, garlic, diced onion, tomato, mixed seasoning and hot pepper sauce.

Allow the pot to boil on high heat source until the meat is tender and butter beans mashes soft to finger pressure then turn down the heat to medium.

Divide the breadfruit into four boats, peal off the outer skin then separate the outer half inch of flesh from the guts. Wash the boats of edible breadfruit, introduce them to the pot and continue boiling.

Combine the flour, corn meal and baking powder, together with ¼ teaspoon of salt, the remainder of vegetable oil and sufficient water, then kneed the mixture into tight, firm dough. Divide the dough into four lumps. Cut the bacon fat into four parts. Insert each bacon part into the centre of one dough lump. Roll each combination 'dough-bacon' between hands before moulding into preferred dumpling shapes then add to the boiling pot.

Peel the ground provisions, cut each type into four parts, wash them and add to the boiling pot.

The remaining ingredients should then be introduced to the stew then bring to the boil at reduced heat for a further thirty minutes or until the various ground provisions are soft when pierced and the dumplings float to the top of the stew.

Serve the stew hot in suitable sized bowls.

Stew with breadfruit on top, served in a bowl.

Sweet & Sour Glazed B'fruit.

Ingredients:

2 Tablespoons of brown sugar.

2 Tablespoons of margarine.

1 Tablespoon lime/lemon juice.

4 Cups of 1 inch cubed breadfruit.

1 Sprig of parsley for garnishing.

1 Teaspoon of salt.

¼ Cup of water.

¼ Cup of vinegar.

12 Toothpicks.

Method:

Wash the 'cubed breadfruit', together with the other ingredients.

Except for the parsley, cook the other ingredients on a high flame/heat with a cover for 5 minutes.

Remove the cover from the pot and allow cooking to continue until the water has evaporated and oil is the only liquid left in the pot, thereby emitting a frying sound.

Turn the burner off then toss the contents around in the cooking pot to give an oily cover to the breadfruit contents.

Mince the parsley, sprinkle over the breadfruit and toss again.

Push one toothpick through the centre of each cube.

The Sweet & Sour glazed breadfruit can then be served, hot or cold.

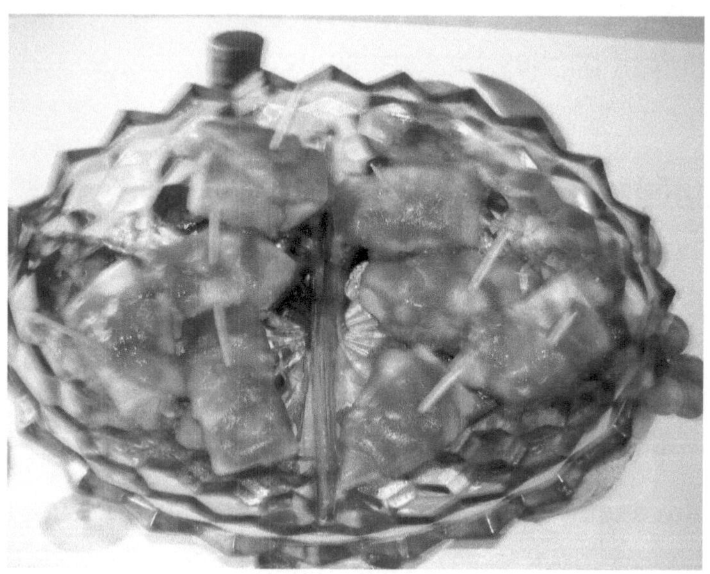

Zesty Cheese Casserole.

Ingredients:

1 Lb. of breadfruit. ¾ Cup of milk.

1 Teaspoon of mustard. 6 Oz's of grated cheese

½ Cup of minced onions and sweet peppers.

Salt and peeper to taste.

Method:

Peel, cook and mash the breadfruit.

Heat the milk then combine it with the other ingredients then to the breadfruit and mix well.

Pour the contents into a greased dish, using a kitchen fork to decorate the top of the mixture.

Sprinkle the top with the grated cheese.

Bake the dish in an oven set to 300 degrees for thirty minutes. By which time the top should be golden brown and the cheese melted.

Summary;

'Breadfruit Recipes' were developed thereby deny the notion that only a few prescribed ways of cooking breadfruit exist. This book demonstrates that with imagination, the fruit can be adapted to uses traditionally associated with the potato, pasta and even flour dishes. The inventive spirit, senses of adventure and willingness to try 'something new' are the only barriers that stand in the way of frontiers to culinary adventures and discoveries. It is felt that there are other, yet untested ideas, which can be adapted and made applicable to using the breadfruit as the basis to their creations. In that sense, this need not be the finality of the experiment and a sequel is not beyond the bounds of the developer's inventive genius.

S. Nathan,
Author.

www.ingramcontent.com/pod-product-compliance
Ingram Content Group UK Ltd.
Pitfield, Milton Keynes, MK11 3LW, UK
UKHW040557210726
13854UKWH00007B/1222

9 780557 127375